Nelson Mandela

By Karima Grant

Consultant
Nanci R. Vargus, EdD
Assistant Professor of Literacy
University of Indianapolis
Indianapolis, Indiana

Children's Press®
A Division of Scholastic Inc.
New York   Toronto   London   Auckland   Sydney
Mexico City   New Delhi   Hong Kong
Danbury, Connecticut

Designer: Herman Adler Design
Photo Researcher: Caroline Anderson
The photo on the cover shows Nelson Mandela.

Library of Congress Cataloging-in-Publication Data

Grant, Karima, 1972–
 Nelson Mandela / by Karima Grant.
    p. cm. — (Rookie biographies)
 Includes index.
 ISBN 0-516-25270-4 (lib. bdg.)   0-516-25537-1 (pbk.)
 1. Mandela, Nelson, 1918– —Juvenile literature. 2. Presidents—South Africa—
Biography—Juvenile literature. I. Title. II. Rookie biography.
 DT1974.G73 2005
 968.06'5'092—dc22   2005004029

CHILDREN'S PRESS, and ROOKIE BIOGRAPHIES®, and associated
logos are trademarks and/or registered trademarks of Scholastic Library
Publishing. SCHOLASTIC and associated logos are trademarks and/or
registered trademarks of Scholastic Inc.

1 2 3 4 5 6 7 8 9 10 R 14 13 12 11 10 09 08 07 06 05

Names mean a lot. When Nelson Mandela was a boy, his nickname was Rolihlahla. It means "troublemaker."

Nelson Mandela was born on July 18, 1918. He was born in Transkei, South Africa. Transkei was a land just for black people.

South Africa had laws called apartheid.

Apartheid meant black people had to live separate from white people. They could not travel where they wanted. They could not vote.

Mandela went to a school for black students. In school, the teachers taught that apartheid was good. Mandela did not agree.

Mandela went to other schools.
He became a lawyer. He helped
many black people fight the
unfair laws. He promised
that one day they would
end apartheid.

11

The South African government did not like Nelson Mandela. They did not want to end apartheid. They put him in jail several times.

Many people listened to Nelson Mandela. They wanted to end apartheid, too. Mandela became popular.

15

The government put Mandela in jail again. Mandela did not care. He still believed apartheid was unfair. He wanted it to end.

Mandela sewed his own clothes while in prison.

Mandela stayed in jail for 27 years. He woke up early each day. He exercised. He read many books. He wrote speeches against apartheid.

People around the world read Mandela's speeches. They believed that apartheid should end. They wrote letters. They made calls to the government. They wanted Nelson Mandela out of jail.

21

In 1990, the government let Nelson go. They agreed to end apartheid. They said black people could vote.

The people voted for Nelson Mandela. He became the first black president of South Africa.

Mandela loves to talk to children. He tells them they must never give up on their dreams. They must always believe in themselves and their ideas.

Nelson Mandela did make trouble. But the trouble he made changed South Africa forever.

Words You Know

apartheid

children

jail

President Mandela   sewing

voting

31

Index

About the Author

Karima Grant lives in Dakar, Senegal, with her husband and three children. One of the prettiest streets in Dakar is named after Nelson Mandela. In addition to writing books for children and adults, Karima also teaches literature to Senegalese students.

Photo Credits

Photographs © 2005: AP/Wide World Photos/John Parkin: 3, 30 top left, 31 top left; Corbis Images/David Turnley: cover; Getty Images: 26, 30 top right (Lee Celano), 4, 8 (Alexander Joe), 22 (Trevor Samson); Hulton|Archive/Getty Images: 18, 31 top right (Express Newspapers), 16; Magnum Photos: 7, 11, 15, 21 (Ian Berry), 12, 30 bottom (Steve McCurry); The Image Works/Allan Tannenbaum: 29; Time Life Pictures/Getty Images/William F. Campbell: 25, 31 bottom.